THE MOVIE

THANKS TO:
Cast & Crew, Jennie Roberts (Hair), Karin Darnell (Make-Up), Alan Underwood and all the guys at M & A Security
and Crawfords, Camilla Howarth, Rachel Pinfold, Jenny Damen, Lynne Dalziel, Catri Drummond, and everyone else
at 19 Management. Cressida Dawson, Gerrard Tyrrell, the guys at React and Jake Lingwood at Ebury Press.

INTERVIEWS:
Rebecca Cripps

SPICE GIRLS' MANAGEMENT:
Simon Fuller at 19 Management

© 1997 by Five Girls Ltd.

Published by **Three Rivers Press**,
a division of **Crown Publishers**, Inc.,
201 East 50th Street, New York, NY 10022.
Member of the Crown Publishing Group.

Originally published in Great Britain by **Ebury Press** in 1997.

Random House, Inc. New York, Toronto, London, Sydney, Auckland
www.randomhouse.com

THREE RIVERS PRESS and colophon are trademarks of Crown Publishers, Inc.

Printed in USA

Designed by **React**

Library of Congress Cataloging-in-Publication Data is available upon request.

ISBN 0-609-80338-7

10 9 8 7 6

THE MOVIE

BY THE SPICE GIRLS

THREE RIVERS PRESS

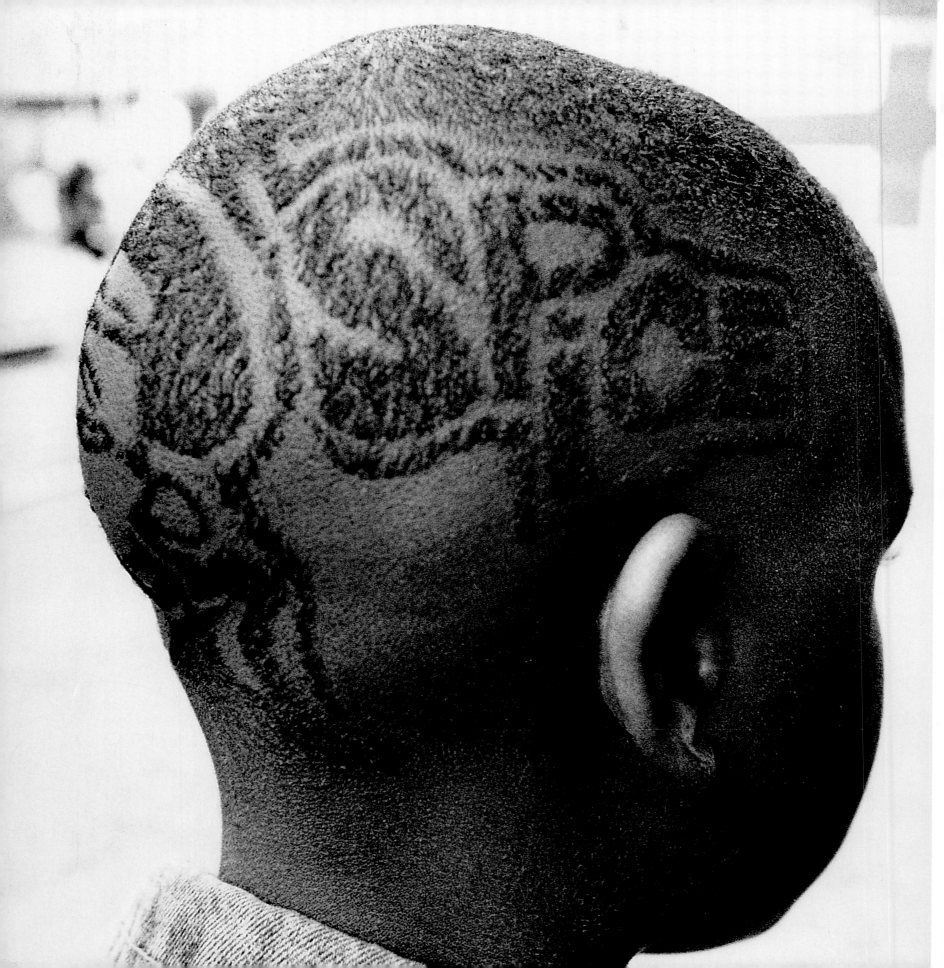

SPICEWORLD, THE MOVIE, chronicles a busy week in the lives of pop's latest and biggest phenomenon – the Spice Girls. It follows them on their hectic schedule of performances, band rehearsals, recording sessions, press conferences, photo shoots and interviews in the days leading up to their first ever live concert. Packed with music, energy, laughter, chaos and Girl Power, Spiceworld is the only place to get to know the real Spice Girls and the characters behind their stage nicknames of Baby, Scary, Posh, Sporty and Ginger.

At the beginning of the film, the Spice Girls are under enormous pressure. After No. 1 hits all over the world and a sensationally successful album, the media spotlight has never been more intense and everyone wants a piece of them, from tabloid journalists to fans. A documentary crew is following them around, desperately trying to capture their lives behind the scenes. Their road manager tells them, 'You don't have a life, you have a schedule!'

But what they want is to be true to themselves and the people who really matter, like their best and oldest friend, Nicola, who asks them all to be godmothers to her unborn child.

The movie starts with a very special performance on *Top of the Pops* and it's non-stop from there on. Then, on the eve of their debut live performance, disaster strikes when the Girls have a row with their road manager and stomp out of rehearsals, threatening not to turn up for the gig. That night, they decide to go out and party with Nicola, only to end up in hospital watching her give birth! Will they make it to the gig? Despite being chased by a photographer who has been hired by an evil media baron to bring them down, the Spice Girls arrive in the nick of time to give a stunning performance at the Albert Hall.

Introducing the

Spice Girls

Mel C gets her nickname for her sporty clothes and her undivided loyalty to Liverpool FC.

'My character in the film is very close to the real me, although obviously I'm a bit more animated because I'm in front of a camera. It's kind of me when I'm trying to be funny. You see, I've got this little personality that comes out sometimes when I think I'm really funny – but no one else seems to appreciate it! That's not true, actually – Mel B thinks I'm funny. (We stick up for each other because we're both from up North.)'

Scary by name, scary by nature, Mel B lives up to her nickname and is the loudest, most up-front example of Girl Power in action. She's the one with the pierced tongue and zebra suits.

'The character I play is quite close to the real me. Everyone's made up of different parts, and the loud, energetic part of me was the bit that came out in the film. I'm the one who says, "Don't do that! Let's do this! Come on!"'

Emma is the little, innocent one. Or is she?
In one scene the rest of the band teases her about how she can get
away with anything because she's so sweet. And they should know –
her cute smile has got them out of trouble hundreds of times!

'If I'd been playing someone else, I suppose I would have done loads of research into how my character would walk or talk, but because I was playing myself, I just had to go into work and be me. I found it all very natural. Obviously I had to go through my scenes and lines and think to myself, "How would I say that?" But that was about it.'

Geri's the temptress with a sense of humour and lashings of attitude.
Witty, glamorous and outspoken, she's also got a heart of gold.

'The part I played was true to me, but obviously you've got different layers to your character and you don't want to reveal all of them. It's not the whole picture. I didn't really do that much preparation, but as we got further into the film, I could feel whether I was being true to my character.'

Sophisticated and a little shy, Victoria sends herself up in the film by pretending that all she thinks about is clothes. She's the classy one – the ultimate Gucci Girl – with a great line in deadpan humour.

'I'd say that the character I play in the film is very much like me. Everyone seems to think that I'm majorly moody and I don't ever speak and I've got no personality whatsoever, but in the film a little bit more of my personality is showing than usual. It is exaggerated slightly, but I get quite a few good lines in it and that really is me – I've got a very dry sense of humour. We know the writer quite well and he sees that side of me, so a lot of my part was written for me by him, but we had ideas as we went along actually doing the scenes and I added in quite a few bits.'

The Spiceworld Script

Geri: 'I worked very closely with Kim Fuller on the script for about two months before we started shooting. Even when I was on holiday in Bali I was spending hours on the phone trying to get it all sorted out and make sure that it was right. By the time we started, it was almost perfect. Okay, everyone changed a couple of words here and there, but no one felt that the situations they were in were wrong. That was the main thing.'

Mel B: 'We all had quite a lot of impact on the script, individually and collectively. It was important to have input because we were the ones having to act the parts and we needed to believe in what we were saying so that we could get into it. Most of the time I looked through the scenes for the next day at night in bed, but sometimes I'd just give it a quick look through and then vibe off it. It wasn't the kind of script you have to stick to word for word, so it was quite flexible.

'A lot of the stories in the film were translated from events that actually happened to us. We told Kim all our stories and spent some time with him so he could really get to know us, and he took bits from all of us and linked it all up. He knows what we like and don't like, so we trusted him to get on with it.'

Mel C: 'We've known Kim Fuller, the writer, for a long time and he's a really good friend of ours. We've spent a lot of time chatting with him over the years and we've always told him our funny little stories and stuff, so he found it easy to write in our words and in our characters. Still, we were always changing our lines, which drove everyone else mad. But you need to be comfortable with what you're saying – otherwise it's going to feel stiff. So we changed lines round and popped in words here and there – nothing major.'

Kim Fuller, film writer: 'I really worked hard to make the Girls sound as natural as possible in the film. First I wrote reams and reams of dialogue with them just talking about anything, from boyfriends to television. I was just making it all up, but I tried to think of them individually as I wrote each line. Obviously I was aware of their stereotypes, but that's more of a visual thing in the end. In terms of character you've got to find another attitude to go with that. I know them quite well, so it wasn't massively difficult. And as time went on, I started finding that I could write lines that sounded convincingly like them.

'In a way, I tried to find broader identities for the Girls in the film. For example, Victoria's always talking about clothes and I found quite a self-parodying way of doing that. In real life, she's fairly self-mocking. She's not really posh posh and she knows that, so when we had a scene when the others are talking about something, her angle would always be fashion.

For instance, when the girls are describing the aliens they've met to Clifford (their road manager) and telling him how they're all green and furry, Victoria says, "And they were wearing these cheap-looking coats!"

'At the other side of the scale, you've got, say, Mel C. When I wanted a scene to have some emotional impact, she'd be the one to say, "You can't do this, what about our fans? We've got to look after our fans," or something like that. I hoped the audience would believe in her emotionally, because she's stronger in that way. So you expect a comment about fashion from Victoria and something far less superficial from Mel C.

'And in between them is Emma. Emma's hook is the Baby Spice thing, although in the film she's not a real baby, Baby Spice. The joke is that she plays on that Baby Spice thing to get the band out of trouble. There are a couple of moments where she's pushed forward to smile and get them out of a tight spot. At one point Emma says, "Am I always going to be Baby Spice even when I'm thirty?" But she's quite feisty too. She can be quite strong, as you can see when she's attacking Clifford at the end of the film.

'Mel Brown is all about big attitude, so she's always coming in and sorting people out. At one point she tells Clifford, "You're in for it now, you're in trouble!" She's not so worried about what people think – she's forceful and strong. There's one scene where there's a flashback and the Girls are going to sing "Wannabe" to a chap in a coffee bar. When he says, "I don't know if I want to hear it, actually," Mel B immediately says, "Well, just sit down there and listen, 'cause you're gonna hear it anyway!" Then she just turns it on and you know that's it. Full stop. She's also the one who's always asking "Are we there yet?", "When are we going to get there?", "How much further?" and "What are we doing now?"

'With Geri, we found a hook for her based on how she's always heard about something somewhere and always read about something somewhere. So she's always saying, "Apparently, in this book that I read..." She's also the one who will fight for what she believes in and that will sometimes get her into trouble. At the start of the film she's reading horoscopes. Emma says, "I don't believe in horoscopes," and Geri says, "Well, that's because you're Aquarius!"

'I think the Girls have got good comic abilities. They can all deliver a line and make it funny. But it's hard to write scenes with five main characters in them. Once I had found an angle on them individually, I then had to work out what to do with them. Then I decided to make it a few days in their life. I wanted to show that franticness of it all – one minute doing an interview, another minute doing an appearance, then whizzing off to another country to do a gig, then whizzing back.

'The script took about a year, which is actually quite quick. Normally it's a two-year process to get something up on screen. Then, when we were actually shooting, every day I'd go in with that day's pages and I'd sit with them and we'd talk it through. One of the girls might say, "I don't want to say that," or "How about if I say this?" and then I'd re-write it that day, which drove the continuity girl crazy. Then we'd go on the set and run it through a few times and maybe add a few more lines there or take some away, working with the director, Bob Spiers. So it was a constant rolling process.

'I talked to them about the script as it was being written, particularly to Geri, who discussed it with the others. In my mind I saw a mix of *A Hard Day's Night* and *Spinal Tap*. In other words I didn't want a big high-concept narrative, where they go on a heist, get kidnapped and it ends in a big chase. I felt it would be better if it was based around the Girls' characters, because that would be more effective in the end. And also I wasn't sure, as they weren't, about their individual acting ranges and strengths, so I didn't want them to have to be massively different to how they actually are.

'For a while I thought I had too many things in there,

what with the press following them, the writer pitching for a Spice Girls' film, their friend Nicola, and the gig. That's four strands, but I feel it works.

'It's a very fast-moving film with loads of different characters. I wanted to cast good actors, so once we'd got Richard E [Grant] and Alan Cumming, who isn't massively famous although he's a great actor, we started building up a cred. You wouldn't have thought you'd get Roger Moore to do a Spice Girls' film, for example, but he did it.

'People are always going on about the svengali behind the Spice Girls, but obviously the Richard E character wouldn't carry that because he's much too fallible and mad. I wanted the real power to be someone you don't see, like in Bond films, where the cat is being stroked. Then Simon thought, what about Roger Moore, because if you're going to include that role, it has to be played by someone really famous. Roger's character is very weird and talks a load of nonsense – the joke is that his policy with the Girls is based on some really obscure philosophy. When Roger came in to shoot his scenes, I sat in the dressing room with him and asked if he liked the script. He said he thought it was funny – "It's just a Buddhist type thing, isn't it?" He knew exactly how to do it – totally deadpan and straight.

'Clare Rushbrook is also great. Some of the casting happened quite late, even while we were filming. First Jools Holland was well up for it, and then probably the word went around a bit. It was quite reassuring that people were agreeing to be in the film after they'd read the script! Suddenly everyone wanted to be in it and we kept getting phonecalls from celebrities.

'The Girls were very bubbly and fun to work with. There were times when they messed around a lot, but it wasn't a problem. Most of the time they were very disciplined, because they are absolute professionals, especially considering that they'd not done a film before and they were in make-up for two or three hours every day, starting at six in the morning. They had a laugh, ribbed the crew and messed about with Richard E a lot. My job on set was really to help Bob to keep them focused on the lines and deliver them in the right way. We all had a great time doing it.'

The Spice

B U S

The Spice Bus is a customised double-decker bus painted in Union Jack colours. It's a bit like Dr Who's Tardis – much bigger on the inside than the outside, luxuriously carpeted, with five individual sections for each Spice Girl on the lower deck. Each section has been fitted out to suit each girl's character.

Emma's part of the bus is filled with toys and fluffy animals, a slide and a swing. This is where Baby Spice comes to play when she's got time off from her busy schedule.

'It's quite true to life, really, because at home I've got lots of teddies and cuddly toys. Sometimes I sleep with a couple of them, but sometimes they get on my nerves and I throw them out!'

Mel B's section has a mystical, gothic feel to it and is decorated with leopardskin throws and oriental wall hangings. This is where Scary Spice retreats for peace, quiet and meditation.

'I've got leopardskin everything in my bedroom at home – leopardskin sheets, wall hangings and bedcovers. I've also got a meditation chair, which is very calming.'

Geri's area of the bus is done up in bright colours like a sixties pad, with posters of Charlie's Angels on the walls. It's a retro haven and the ideal place for Ginger Spice to contemplate life and be inspired.

'I'm really into retro, especially stuff from the fifties and sixties.'

Mel C has an exercise bike in her section and the walls are plastered with posters of Liverpool FC. Here Mel C works out her excess energy and dreams of FA Cup success.
'I get grumpy if I don't have a work-out in the morning. Even when I'm tired, doing a workout makes me feel energised and

psyched up for the rest of the day – ready to take on the world!'
Victoria's room is chic, sleek and Vogue-ish, with a long rail of expensive clothes (mainly little black dresses made by Gucci). This is where Posh Spice plans her wardrobe and indulges her designer dreams.

'I like being smart and I love dressing up. My favourite shops are Prada and Gucci – where else?'

There is also a kitchen area on the bus, with food and drink vending machines. On the second level of the bus is Clifford's office, where the road manager's phones are constantly ringing

'Oh no! It's the Rozzers!'

and faxes spew out endless sheets of paper. Clifford's window looks down on to the lower deck, where the Girls' rooms are.

Geri: 'It's a bizarre set design, with five sections each catering to each girl's personality – Emma's is a playground, Mel C's is a gym and mine has a pair of lips for an armchair. It's quite freaky, because when I saw the prototype months before the film started, it was about ten inches high! The only problem with the real thing is that there's no air conditioning and it's sweltering in there.'

Driven by Dennis (played by Meat Loaf), the Spice Bus takes the girls from rehearsals to press conferences via magazine shoots, recording studios and parties. At one point, in an emergency, Victoria takes the wheel of the Spice Bus, puts her foot down and bombs through the streets of London. As she approaches Tower Bridge, it starts to open. Will she make it across?

Victoria: 'In real life I really do drive that way, like a bit of a nutter. In fact, the other day I got pulled over for speeding by an undercover police car. It was really early in the morning and I had my hair tied up in a ponytail and secured with a G-string (like you do). I had a big baggy jumper on, no shorts or skirt and no shoes or socks, so I looked nothing like me. They asked me to get in their car to watch the video of how fast I was going. I said, "Actually, I don't really want to see it. Just give me the points and I'll go." But they insisted I get into their car, so I did.

'Eventually I said, "Look, I'm a Spice Girl and I'm late for work." They thought I was lying because I just looked like a normal person, even though I was sitting there saying, "Yeah, I've got Girl Power! I'm a Spice Girl!" They told me to prove it. So I had to take my hair out of the size 8–10 M&S knickers that I had hanging out of my head, let my bob down, take off my glasses and start posing like I do at photo shoots. They said, "Oh, you're our favourite one! We've stuck you over Jet from the Gladiators." In the end I gave them loads of autographs and they let me off, which was incredibly lucky. I won't be driving too fast again, that's for sure!'

Geri: 'It was my idea for Victoria to speed off in the bus. I thought it was a really good idea for her to do that because for most of the film she plays a bit of a one-dimensional character, who's very tight-lipped. Then right at the end she says, "Hold on to your knickers, girls!" and goes for it, speeding off in the bus.'

Kim Fuller: 'I thought the Girls should have a Spicemobile. We thought *of Summer Holiday* and decided it should be a bus that was bigger on the inside than it is on the outside. The designer did a great job with it.'

Clifford

The Spice Girls' Road Manager

Clifford (played by Richard E Grant) answers to the Chief (played by Roger Moore). It is obvious that the Chief is the real power behind the Spice Girls, but since he also appears to be completely nuts, it is down to Clifford to deal with the day-to-day Spice schedule. Clifford seems hard-bitten, cynical and weary of life, but he still takes his job extremely seriously.

Just before the Girls break free for an adventure on the river, Victoria describes him as 'a fascist, tyrant dictator slave-driver ordering us about all day'.

There are at least three sides to his job: making sure the Girls work hard; stopping the press from taking photos up anyone's skirts; and attempting to keep the showers on the Spice Bus in working order.

 Clifford: *Well done girls, excellent performance.*
Mel B: *How do you know, Clifford? You weren't even watching.*
Clifford: *I sensed the vibes. I have an excellent vibe sensor –* (pointing to his forehead) *– right here.*

Emma: *He doesn't love us any more.*
Clifford: *Yes I do. I love you like a wildebeest loves five lionesses chewing at his legs.*
Geri: *Well, that's a start.*

Kim Fuller: 'I thought that having a manager figure was important. I wanted somebody for them to fight against – a straight man in a way, but also mad. I didn't want to show them cracking up with the pressure, because they're not cracking up in real life, but I wanted to show how much pressure they're living with through Clifford, who's on the edge of a nervous breakdown the whole time. Their real manager, Simon Fuller, is far more laid back than that, of course.

'I thought of Richard E Grant because I had worked with him before and had always liked that suppressed manicness that he does. I wrote the part of Clifford with him in mind. Clifford provides some of the drama, because he's always trying to control the Girls and make them work hard and turn up on time.'

Geri's Diary

Monday **9 June** Call time **7.45am**

It's the first day of shooting. There is a subtle feeling of nerves and anticipation about what the day ahead will bring. We are shooting the Poirot scene with Emma, who was a little anxious about going first. But she'll be fine. The rest of us shared our feelings about the day ahead. It's good to know you're not alone.

Well, the first day is over. After we'd had our make-up and hair done and got into costume, we had a little rehearsal and began shooting. It's a relief that those early nerves have disappeared.

Richard E Grant was fab, funny, professional and very inspiring as an actor. He immediately rushed over with a warm hello! He was taking snaps and shooting film footie for his eight-year-old daughter. Clare Rushbrook, who plays Deborah (our real-life PA Camilla) was very sweet. It was quite mad – she'd got the part to a T.

Poor Emma had a real early start, as she was the first on set filming her Poirot scene with Hugh Laurie, who is an awfully nice chap. And she wasn't happy at the thought of another

early start – she was picked up at 5am today and is scheduled to do so again tomorrow.

Our first collective scene was around the dinner table at the mansion, where Clifford reveals his personal life. We all really got into it, like ducks to water. It was highly enjoyable. We had to be shot from many angles and I was particularly proud of my sad face when Clifford was telling his tale of woe. Hey! We're darling luvvie actors now!

Emma: 'I hated the early mornings on the film. I'm the kind of person who likes getting up late and going to bed late. Still, it was really exciting to be doing something so different.'

Mel B: 'Richard E Grant was fantastic to work with. He's very flirtatious and charming, and he's got a huge vocabulary. He's very precise with the way he uses words and he's an amazing man to watch – it's like he's always on show when he's with

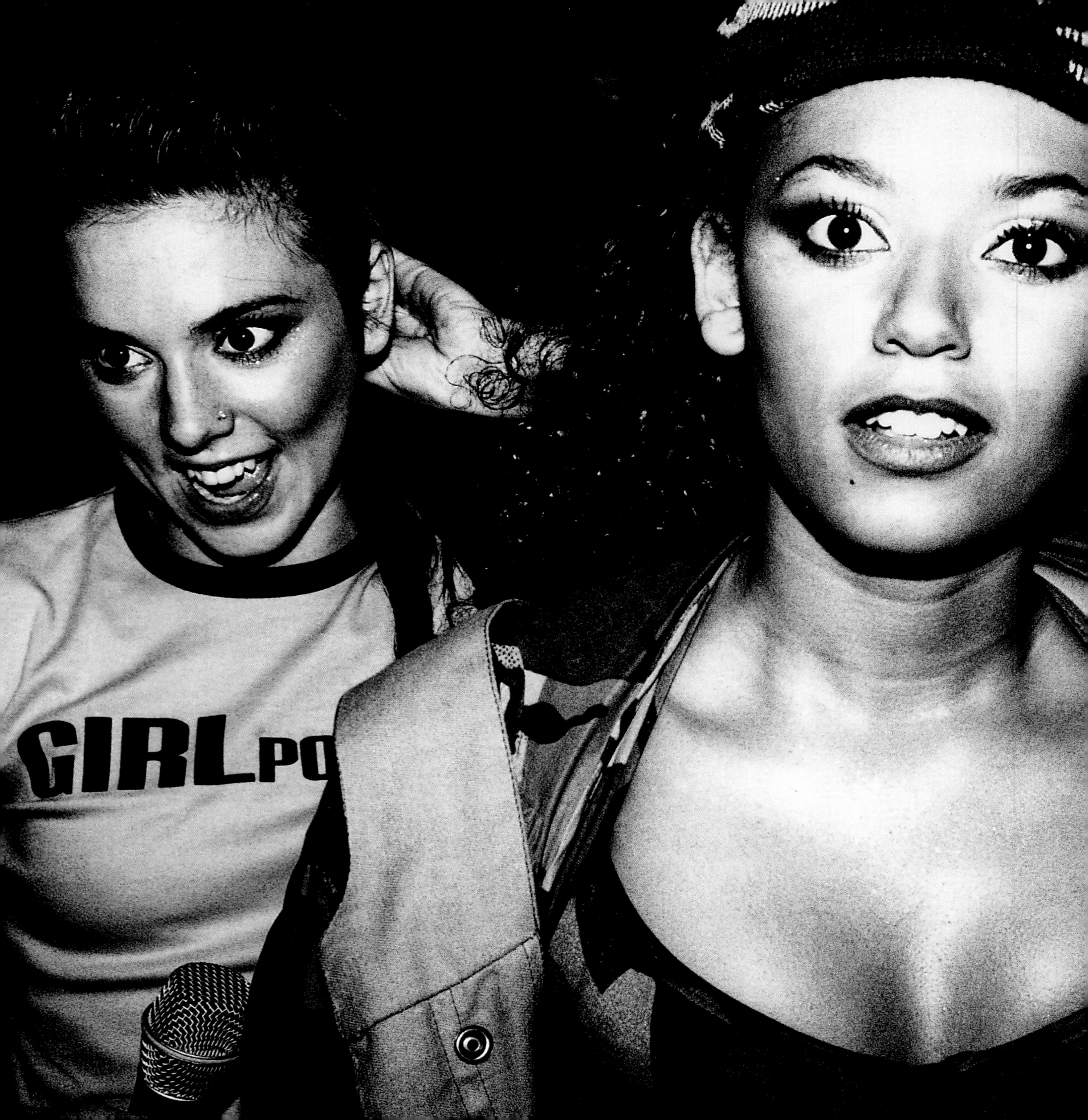
GIRLPO

you, as though he's in the film all the time. When you have a chat with him, he'll suddenly start interviewing you and joking around. He's quite hyperactive, really.'

Mel C: 'I was very nervous at the start of the film because the only acting I'd ever done before was in school plays. I was a bit anxious about doing it professionally, especially with so many fantastic actors, so the first day was really daunting. But it was great. Richard E Grant was really, really sweet. He was incredibly helpful and made us feel really at ease. He was good fun, too. He makes us laugh. The crew made it easy, too, so once we'd started, it was fine and we just had a laugh. It's the same with everything – because there are five of us all together, we're all in the same position and we've got each other for support.'

Emma: 'We've got loads of in-jokes from the film that come out here and there. One of them is: "Whippet!" That's from "You've got to do it like a whippet", which is something Richard E Grant had a habit of standing up and saying really loudly for a laugh.'

Victoria: 'We did quite a lot of messing around when Richard E Grant was on set. He's so funny that you just can't help having a laugh with him.'

Mel B: 'The first scene we filmed was round the table at Clifford's mansion. I wasn't so much nervous as excited. It was like, "We're actually doing it now!" We knew our lines but we worked in some spontaneity, which was good because it allowed us to feel a little bit more relaxed about it all. It was exciting when we heard the director say "Lights! Camera! Action!" for the first time. We felt like little kids – it was funny. It was good fun mixing with so many actors and it was nice to know that at the end of the day, they're all quite normal as well, although there are a lot more luvvies in the acting world than in music.'

Victoria: 'I didn't really prepare for the film because I was playing myself. To be quite honest, I'm a real fretter and if I start thinking too much about something I'll start worrying about it and then I'll make myself ill. So I tried not to think about it too much in advance. Obviously I had to learn my lines, but often I didn't do that until the day we were shooting that scene.'

Fame and

the Media

Central to the plot of Spiceworld are the mischievous attempts by tabloid newspaper editor, Kevin McMaxford (played by Barry Humphries), to ruin the Spice Girls' careers. McMaxford is sick of good news about the Spice Girls. He wants a new kind of Spice splash – bad news.

McMaxford: *I want their dreams shattered, Brad. I want the ground to crack and a huge yawning chasm to open up beneath them. I want them destroyed.*
Another crack of thunder, then rain starts falling.
McMaxford: *Who's going to help me, Brad? Who's going to help me take on Girl Power and bring it crashing to the ground?*

McMaxford puts Damien, a paparazzi photographer (played by Richard O'Brien) on the case. Damien is a photographer version of an SAS undercover counter-surveillance expert. Under his coat, half a dozen cameras clink together. Damien follows the Girls around trying to pick up negative newsworthy nuggets. At one point he pops out of a toilet in the middle of the night at

It's quite funny how we're driven such a short distance from our winnibago to the set, so that the paparazzi hiding in the bushes don't snap us!

Today we shot the bedroom scene. It was quite hilarious pretending to be really scared. Creeping down the corridor and bumping into one another was very funny. I was tripping over my Babs Windsor nightie and trying not to laugh at Mel B – oh, and trying not to stare straight into camera! A good day and not too long.

During a visit from their heavily-pregnant friend Nicola, the Spice Girls imagine the day when they too will be mothers.

the house where they're staying. Sensing the intrusion, they all wake up and run into each other's rooms. Later Damien overhears them discussing their imminent live concert.

Tuesday, 10 June
Once again we're shooting at the big manor house in Guildford. (I'd love to live there.)
We're being plagued by the press. Some of them were so desperate to get a scoop that they disguised themselves as a panto horse. They even tried to fake a story by getting a security guard in a scuffle.

Wednesday, 11 June
BATTERSEA PARK SET-UP.
Our first scene was a flash-forward to our futures – as mothers – which was absolutely hilarious. We all looked wicked. Mel B was dressed up like an African mama, Emma looked the perfect wife – butter wouldn't melt in her mouth, Victoria was a drunken Joan Collins, Mel C was Waynetta in a fat suit and I was just a glamorous Hilda. The Dream Boys came down with their fake tans – ugh! – and there were paparazzi waiting in the trees.

Emma: 'I look just like my mother in this scene! That's probably what she looked like when she was preggers with me. I thought I looked quite young, like a teenage mum. The scene looks forward to the day when we're mums and mums-to-be. It was so funny. Vicky's actually going to be like that when she's older – all drunk and frowsy. She says, "Thank god for boarding school – I only see mine once a month."

'I'm heavily pregnant and suffering from a really bad back. Mel B says, "I don't know why you're having another one – you've already had six," and I say, "Is it six?" Then I say something like, "They're so cute when they're younger, and then they grow up to be right little bleeders." I'm one of those mums who has kids because they're so sweet as babies.'

Everywhere the Spice Girls go in *Spiceworld*, there are fans and reporters following them. To make things worse, Clifford allows a hopeless documentary maker called Piers (played by Alan Cumming) to make a behind-the-scenes film about the Girls' lives. Piers is often in the wrong place at the wrong time and he's never really able to keep up with his subjects. At one point he tries to follow them on a mad adventure down the River Thames, but his boat is such a dud that he's left miles behind. This fast-action, stunt-filled scene in which at least five people fall in the river, was partly filmed in London's Docklands.

Sunday, 15 June
Hideous morning start. Picked up at 6.30am! It was quite

Wednesday, 11 June cont'd
Then we did the evening scene in the park, which was quite moving. It's the scene where we're reminiscing and talking about whether the band is going to last. It was kind of coincidental when a boat went down the river behind us playing 'Get Into The Groove', which was a big hit from *Desperately Seeking Susan*. Could this film be a smash hit like that? We are getting better and better. A real laugh.

bizarre seeing clubbers going home just as I was going to work. Those were the days, eh?

Everyone felt totally exhausted. We were filming the boat scene at Docklands. Loads of kids and media frenzy. It's been quite laborious shooting the same sequences over and over again, getting on and off a bus and boat. The real drama is in not falling in the river, as apparently you can catch 'Wills disease', which is not a pretty sight – flesh falling off and convulsions. Nice.

We amused ourselves with Mark, one of our bodyguards, who does a great Grant Mitchell. I'm in a charming little sailor's

with two little kids, wearing our lifejackets. (Billy from EastEnders looks like a mini Mel B.) Fans are hanging out everywhere. 'Will you kiss my baby?' says one mum. This seems a very attractive idea – the kid has a nice green bogey hanging out of its nose and I don't think he even knows who we are!

While they're on a trip with two young competition winners on the Spice Bus, the Girls get restless. Suddenly out of the window Mel B sees a speedboat moored on the bank of a Docklands private lake.

 Mel B (confidentially, to the others) *Hey, when I say go, let's go.*
The bus stops in traffic.
Mel B (cont'd) *Let's go!*

Mel B: 'I didn't have to prepare much for the film. I didn't find the acting difficult because I did drama at college. I found I just went on set and did it. I never got too worked up about it – I just did it to the best of my ability. I enjoyed myself – I always think you do things better when you're having a laugh at the same time. It's not good to put loads of pressure on yourself and start panicking. I went with the flow.'

 EXT. DOCKLANDS BAY
The girls and kids bundle out of the bus and start running along towards the water. Clifford and Deborah walk after them.
Clifford: *Would anyone like to tell me where they're going?*
Deborah: *They're being spontaneous.*
Clifford: *I told them if they want to be spontaneous, they'd have to clear it with me first.*
A large speedboat ploughs through the waves, driven by a young guy. The girls and kids wear lifejackets and hang on as the spray flies up around them. They're having a great time dancing and singing a medley of old songs.

outfit – I always go overboard with my outfits! Filming was cut short due to weather conditions.

We also met the actor Alan Cumming, who plays a quirky news guy accompanied by a fat sound man and a hunky documentary camera man. They follow us in the slow long boat, looking like the Three Stooges. Cumming keeps on doing '2 Become 1' impressions.

Monday, 16 June
Another gruesome early start. None of us come alive until late afternoon. It's now pouring down with rain. We are all vegging in the winnibago and have been over-indulging on the catering. Double helpings of Banoffee Pie. Victoria has fruit poisoning. The hanging around leaves us with no obstacle to our unhealthy obsession with dates. We spent ages waiting in an ambulance

Tuesday, 17 June
STUNT DAY
After two days of loads of waiting around, this was fun. We whipped up and down the docks in a very flashy speed boat in a scene where we're thrown left and right at high speed. Take one: I land in Mel B's crotch – a very enviable position!!

(Although I did crack my neck.) Take two: I land on Emma's recently broken wrist. Take three: I almost fly overboard. Oh no! Wills disease!! But I am saved.

There were lots of spectators round the docks, including some nice builders. 'Show us your builders' bums!' I shout. Sure enough, a line of all-shapes-and-sizes hairy bottoms gets an airing. Not a pretty site!!!

It's girls overboard as Victoria and Melanie get a soaking. Posh is not very happy, as one can imagine – panda eyes and soggy Gucci. Screaming crowds everywhere and paparazzi. *London Tonight* do some sneaky filming when some yuppie guy lets them on to his balcony.

Mel C: 'I never really felt like a movie star, except, perhaps, when we were in our trailers. They were proper winnibagos and looked like hotel suites inside. But most of the time, making the film wasn't at all glamorous. We shot a lot of the scenes outside, so we were always waiting for the rain to stop or the clouds to blow over. It was really frustrating. In the river scene, Victoria and I had to get very wet. It was a freezing day and our clothes were soaking and we had to keep getting wet again and again and again, for hours on end.'

Wednesday, 18 June

Another early start – picked up at 6am. We're ready to go at 9.30am but we don't actually start the stunt sequence until lunchtime, so we're a bit gutted. We end up on this poxy boat for four hours – Mel B, Emma, Mel C and I sit in the cabin for hours, feeling very seasick. As for the stunt guys, there's Victoria's double, who is extremely foxy, an Asian midget who's playing the little boy and a small, stocky woman you wouldn't want to mess with. They all have to fall into the water. Unfortunately they keep getting the timing wrong and have to do it over again, which is a long process because they have to dry off each time.

At one point they are all in the water, including Mel C Sporty's double. Emma, Mel B and I have to lean over the boat screaming at our friends. But by this time we all have cabin fever and we're in hysterical giggles, so we have to cover our faces to mask our laughter. Hopefully we'll look concerned!

After filming we all pile into the portable studio and manage to write a pretty cool song. I wrote some of the lyrics in the back of the car the other night when I was depressed.

Little do we know that it's kicking off bigtime outside the set. Hundreds of kids have accumulated over the day and it's getting rather chaotic as they try and storm the set. The police are called and it's a mini-riot. The mums and dads are not happy about it, as they proudly express on *London Tonight*. We're oblivious to it all as we're singing away at the back of the set. Oh well, another day at the office.

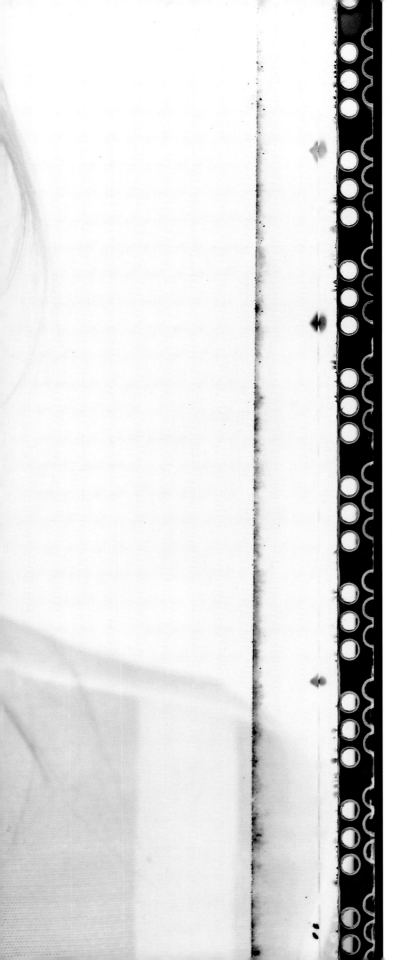

In an early scene, the Spice Girls perform 'Too Much', a track from their new album, on Top of the Pops (TOTP). As they leave the BBC studios, Clifford assures them that they will avoid the crowds outside by leaving by the back door. But when he kicks open the exit door, there is a huge mass of screaming fans jostling to get near the Girls. Immediately the Girls move off in a cluster of chaos until Clifford tries to nudge them on to the Spice Bus and calls out:

 Clifford (v.o.): *All aboard.*
He rings the bell and the bus shoots off. The fans run down the street, yelling and screaming.

Victoria: 'I liked it when we did "Too Much", because I really like the song, we all had nice white dresses on and there's a good dance to it. It's a real feel-good song. We filmed it at *TOTP*, which was nice. We always have a good time when we record *TOTP*.'

Saturday, 21 June, day 7

I would like to say that this morning's pick-up time was positively vile – 5.30am. I got out of bed at 5.35am – well, I refused to conform. That five minutes extra gave me a sense of defiance of time. I flopped into the car still wearing my pyjamas and arrived at the BBC studio extremely crumpled and blurry–eyed.

The first shoot was a complete nightmare because we had limited access to our time in the BBC corridor. I personally thought, hey, this could be any corridor, couldn't it? Anyway, we did a million just-one-more takes for this scene where fans are screaming outside. I'll leave it to your imagination, but reciting the same scene over and over again in front of hysterical eight-year-olds can get to the best of them.

Richard E was on top form today – extremely comical. Our conversations all developed on a downward spiral, using eloquent words like spermatozoa!! It's amazing what keeps one occupied. Andy Coulson, *the Sun*'s Bizarre editor, showed up looking like one of the reservoir media dogs. 'Can I have a part in your movie?' Yeah, right!

After lunch Mr Elton John came down – with a very large entourage, I might add. Elton delivered his witty line with the style of a frisky dandy. But that's another story...

Twelve-hour day – we finished at 6.30pm.

Dressing UP

'Doing the film was like being a kid again, like dressing up in my mum's clothes and high heels and going out in the street with all my mates.' *Mel B*

Sunday, 22 June

Today I get a lie-in – picked up at 6.30am!! Tired but happy.

Today does not feel quite right. Here I am in wardrobe debating latex pants or denim, with my hair in curlers and a shovel of blusher. Here am I when every other 'normal' person is sleeping, watching *Grange Hill* re-runs or eating their Frosties. But I talk myself round by saying that you shouldn't have to conform. So Sunday is meant to be a day of rest. Rest, who needs it? We don't!?

I'm late for our script reading. I enter a very small caravan with the other Spice Girls, Richard E, Clare and Jools Holland, who plays our musical director. Everyone is pretty casual. For five minutes, I am too, but then I yell, 'It's Jools Holland! Sorry, I had to get that out of the way. Now we can begin.' Everything flows and seems pretty cool. Jools is our instant buddy and we volley banter and witty quips all day.

Today was a hard but good day. Have you ever reached that level of tiredness when everything is hilarious? Everyone even finds me funny – they too must be tired. Humour is the best remedy in the world. I cannot stop talking in a broad Scottish accent because the crew are mostly Scots.

Here's a tip: if you need a good-natured crew, then wheel in the Scotsmen. They're cheery and happy, but with a cynical dry edge to keep you on your toes. Finish 8pm – pop star's glamorous lifestyle, eh! I am off home, talking to myself. We contemplate sleeping on set. Why not? Nah, perhaps not.

Monday, 23 June

Tell me why I love Mondays? Pick-up 7am.

Today I was Marilyn and Wonder Woman. Tomorrow – who knows? It was an exhibitionist's dream. I was back in wonderland, making a childish fantasy into reality. As I stood upon the grate, the wind rushed up and almost blew my wig off. The thought dawned on me that here I was, little Geri, dressed as the sexiest woman ever – Marilyn Monroe, for godsake – with a rather large crowd watching. I swiftly tried to bury my nervous awkwardness. 'Happy Birthday Mr President,' I murmured.

Each of us played an icon – Jackie O, a Charlie's Angel, Sandy from *Grease*. I have to say I was absolutely amazed at the transformation in Emma – where's my Baby Spice gone??!

The rain pounded and the press pestered to get that preview. Did we get wet? No! Did they get a preview? Hell, no! (Well I hope not. I suppose they could have been hiding on the rooftops.)

We recorded Gary Glitter's 'C'mon C'mon' and I lost my voice. Wrapped at 8.30pm and went to the studio to rewrite 'Good Times'. Arnie was in town so we sent him a note which read: 'Hello Sexy! We really, really want you in our movie. Cigars free. Kids welcome.' We'll have to wait and see.

Mel B: 'One day I pretended to be Diana Ross. I felt very glamorous in all my sequins. With my hair done like hers and her music playing in the background, I felt quite like her. I couldn't walk in the dress, though. I fell over quite a few times, which was quite comical.'

Kim Fuller: 'I wanted a photosession scene because that's something they do a lot. They came up with the ideas of who they wanted to dress up as, except for the final joke when they dress as each other. I wrote down who would be the biggest contrast to whom, and they went along with it.'

Tuesday, 24 June

LOCATION SMITHFIELD MARKET AND PROTO STUDIOS. CALL TIME 11AM.
Today I was Elvis, the late bloater, and I felt like one in my gaudy jumpsuit and with sideburns painted on – the works. Mel C was David Bowie in one of his eccentric phases – was it Ziggy Stardust? She was sporting an eye patch and an absolutely awful pair of red, skin tight trousers. She looked like an amazing freak. You've got to hand it to her – she's sporty in name, and nature too. She's been such a good sport all the way through this movie. She's made me laugh so much. I was uncontrollable with laughter when we teamed up to do this – Elvis, Bowie and Bob Marley (Mel B). I couldn't keep a straight face. I hope they don't cut it out.

We then all dressed up as each other. I was Mel C and felt fantastic with no platforms on, running around like a little imp. Wicked, although I looked like a street kid of about twelve years old. It was a nice change from propping my boobs up to my chin. But I have to say that Mel C is best at being Mel C!

10pm. We shoot outside Smithfield Meat Market. Big crowd. It feels good, just how you imagine movies are made – stopping traffic, lights, action! The mood is serious and intimate. Still we all have such a laugh with each other. I am labelled "Gumbo of the Day" for cocking my line up. 'I wonder whatever did happen to Bob.' Bob? That's the name of our director, durrr! 'I wonder whatever did happen to Brian.' Sorry!!

The press have shots of me as Marilyn, which is a gutter because it was meant to be a surprise. So they *were* hiding on the rooftop.

Finished at midnight.

Emma: 'It was really cool dressing up as each other. I thought Victoria looked great as me – much better than me, in fact! "Get those socks off, they look better on your legs!" The wig was good as well – I might nick it. I loved playing Mel B. I felt really funky, even though I look a bit bigger than she does. I had really dark make-up on and a dark wig which made my eyes look really blue. It definitely made me act differently – because I was wearing trousers I could dance with my legs apart and be really funky – at least, I thought I was. I think it would drive me mad to be like that all the time, though – shouting and screaming and getting my cleavage out. I'm glad I got to dress up as Mel B because she's so different from me. If I was Geri, it would have been a bit different, but in ways we're quite similar. Sometimes I go for the posh look like Victoria anyway and on my days off I wear trackies and trainers, so being Mel C wouldn't have been such a contrast either. So Mel B was the one I had to be because she looks completely different to me. When they put that wig on me my whole face changed. I tried to get her accent when she says "Oh no!" and I think I got it quite well.

'We chose to dress up as the person we least resembled. If you think about it, Victoria is completely different from me – she would never dress in baby dolls and pigtails – so we picked well. This was one of the best days we had on the film.'

Mel C: 'It was really good fun dressing up all the time. Trying to be Victoria was a bit of nightmare, though. I thought I was going to break her dainty little shoes, walking along like a rugby player in her little dress. I looked dead butch. It was quite funny behind the scenes because you'd go to say something to Emma, but Emma would be Victoria and it would really freak

you out. It was a bit like when we did "Who Do You Think You Are?" with the Sugar Lumps for Comic Relief, when you'd turn round to talk to Victoria and it would be Dawn French!'

Victoria: 'I know what I like to wear, which is a bit of a problem when you take on a role. I didn't feel particularly comfortable the day I had to dress up as a Bond Girl and Jackie O, because the clothes were horrible. They were both glamorous parts, but Jackie's skirts were far too long! I like dressing up in clothes I like – not unflattering sacks. Still, it was really good fun getting into the role for the scene where we dressed up as old bags and each other. It was funny dressing up as Emma in a little pink dress and white shoes and it was interesting seeing Mel C as me – you don't realise what your characteristics really are until someone imitates you.

'I really like make-up and I learnt quite a lot from Karin, our make-up artist during the film. It was interesting to find out how to use make-up for different scenes and situations.'

The night before their live performance, the Girls decide to break free and go clubbing with their friend Nicola.

 EXT. LONDON PARK, NIGHT
    Emma: *The trouble is, we just don't have much time for people anymore.*
    Geri: *Like Nicola.*
    Mel C: *We're supposed to be godmothers to her baby and we haven't spent any time with her at all!*
    Emma: *It's not good enough.*
    Geri: *Why don't we take her out tonight?*
    Mel B: *Yeah, and go really mental.*
    Others: *(excited) Yes. Why not? Great idea.*
    Victoria: *Wait a minute, wait a minute – we're doing a live show tomorrow night – what about that?*
    They think about this.
    Mel C: *And if Clifford thought we'd stayed out all night, he'd go berserk.*
    Others: *Yes, right.*
    Silence, as they sit for a moment, all serious.
    Mel B: *So what are we waiting for?*
    They jump up and run off across the park, whooping with excitement.

Wednesday, 25 June

I woke up aching all over. My body was suffering from the shock of yesterday's activity as Sporty. I'm telling you – you have to be sporty to be Sporty Spice!

Today was the club scene at the Ministry of Sound with over 120 extras. They were a sight for sore eyes – drag queens, PVC, muscle men and babes gyrating everywhere. It felt pretty good as we haven't been clubbing for so long. At last, a mad night out. Okay, so it was acting in the movie, but hey, better than sitting in the winnibago.

I must say our acting is steadily improving. It was a tense scene. I believed it, so hopefully, the audience will too. We had to squeeze in two magazine interviews and one *O-Zone* interview between takes as well as do a mini photo-shoot, have a meeting with accountants and a quick chat with the Grim Reaper, our solicitor who deals with the press. We got our security guards to be the bouncers on the door, which was pretty hilarious. One of them looks just like Grant Mitchell. One bizarre thing: one of the extras was Shadow (the ex-Gladiator shamed in a media scandal). It was rather odd seeing him there, gyrating in his leather. I thought he would growl any minute.

Throughout the film, a Hollywood writer (played by Mark McKinney) and American producer Martin Barnfield (played by George Wendt) pitch ideas for a movie starring the Spice Girls to Clifford. One of the scenes is set in an Italian town, where the Girls are performing a concert and singing Gary Glitter's classic 'D'you Wanna Be In My Gang?' This sequence features the Girls in glitter, the Dream Boys in very little glitter and a surprise appearance by the king of glitter himself.

Saturday, 28 June

LOCATION LIVERPOOL STREET, THE CITY. SHOOTING THE ITALIAN SHOW *BIZARRO* WITH THE DREAM BOYS.

As expected, these tanned tangerine torsos turned up to tantalise. Except they didn't, bless 'em. Nice lads, although I felt a little sorry for them – the innuendoes were non-stop. I suppose it goes with the job. Their manager was Andy Warhol re-incarnated – we have to give him a part in the film. I don't think they realised the gag was on them. The scene was a tribute to tacky Italian TV shows.

Annie Lennox and her kids came down. She is a fine woman and very inspiring.

Luck was on our side after the wettest June – it was raining all week but it didn't rain today and we've finished ahead of schedule! An evening off! Whoopee!

There is a brilliant vibe on the set. There seems to be a real camaraderie among everyone – the director, producers, writers, cameramen, actors, extras, runners, costume and make-up. There's a team spirit of fun. I am really enjoying this adventure. I shall be sad when it's over.

Sunday, 29 June

Glitter power!!

Started 6pm, which was rather cruel. We couldn't get into Sunday relaxing mode knowing we would be working later.

So Glitter Power took off at 8.30pm – *Bizarro*, with the Dream Boys and Gary Glitter! What a showman he is. You have to hand it to the man. He still has that *joie de vivre*. How does he maintain such effervescence? He says, 'It's gotta be from within, man, because everything on the outside tends to droop.' Ooh–er! Even when the cameras weren't rolling Gary was still completely switched on, like a true professional. I was dying to ask how old he was – over sixty? I mean, he did those

OAP travelcard ads. Emma's mum came down and she's a big Gary Glitter fan. She went all giggly when she met him. C'mon C'mon – quite a buzz tonight.

The crowd of Italian extras were excellent. The Dream Boys had their bottoms on display. I think they had numb bums! One of them had spots on his bot – it's nice to know they're not perfect. My two Spanish friends came down as extras. They were hilarious – like kids in a candy shop around all the hustle, bustle and muscle!

Finished 1.30am.

While staying at a spooky-looking Gothic mansion, the Girls end up sleeping in the same bed after they all have the same nightmare about their first live performance. The next day, they laze around on brightly-coloured cushions and discuss the press, Clifford, and the mating habits of certain animals.

Monday, 30 June

A harem of relaxation is the only way to describe today's set – filled with giggles, word play and raucous banter. In the scene we were discussing the idiocy of the tabloid media, which was ironically appropriate as we'd all received another helping over the weekend. Marriages? Romances? The press do seem to have a wild imagination, to say the least. But hey, it's only tomorrow's fish and chip paper!

Richard E was neurotically funny, as usual. Michael Barrymore came in later to do some rehearsing. I think he's going to be brilliant as today we couldn't stop laughing. He was hilarious, marching up and down like a Sergeant dandy on acid.

Today's real highlight was receiving a Blue Peter badge. Katy the babe presenter joined in the rumpus and agreed we deserved one. Mel C had to point out, 'C'mon, we've had four No. 1s and broken the US – isn't that worth one?' 'Oh, all right, then.' So that was quite a thrill after all those years of watching toilet rolls and Goldie. We have a real symbol of childhood and it's a pass to get you anywhere.

We brought in our own caterers, as good food is definitely part of the Spice Girls' lifestyle.

Training at the Dance Camp

'Often if you stop and think about what you're doing, it can freak you out a bit.' *Mel B*

The Spice Girls go for intensive dance training at a 'camp' in the countryside outside London, as part of the preparations for their first ever live performance. Their dance teacher (played by Michael Barrymore) is a loud, barking Sergeant-Major type who tries to alter their dance routines before he sends them on an assault course.

 Sergeant-Major: *They tell me you are the Spice Girls. A successful pop music band. You know something? I don't care! I don't give a flying monkey's uncle who you are, because, to me, you are a bunch of klutzy, clod-hopping puddings! Now pull yourselves together.*
The girls stand to attention. They're dressed in army uniform as if on the parade ground. The Sergeant-Major walks up and down the line.

Tuesday, 1 July
Who won the war, eh? Spice Girls?

Well, we weren't there, but today was combat training. We were all in combat greens, ready for anything or fit for nothing? One way or the other, we were up for it with the wacky

Sergeant–Major Barrymore. It was *The Krypton Factor* on acid.

Mel B looked like she was Public Enemy No. 1, but she was Scaredy Spice today, with the swing jump. Emma was Private Benjamin and totally going for it. Me, I was looking like a cross between an old natural hippy (make love, not war) and Rambo. After a really cool run–up I fell into the water like a real plank. As for Victoria, she wore a little army green dress and attempted the assault course in high heels – I don't think so. I was dead proud as we chanted our way in our stomping boots. We ended the day with a photoshoot and a good old mud fight. A wicked day. Sing it now: 'We're in the army now...' Wahoo!!

Mel C: 'One of our in-jokes from the film came from the Michael Barrymore sketch where he keeps saying, "That is correct." We like that one and use it quite a lot now! It's quite funny, because we're always quoting the film these days.'

Emma: 'A lot of the scenes are true, although perhaps they're shown in a different way. And some of the film has actually come true since we did it – like the scene where we're all at

Spice Camp in a big house, going for dance lessons, which is exactly what we've been doing to prepare for our concerts. Also, one of the women who is helping with our clothes is pregnant and going to have a baby any day now, just like our friend Nicola in the film.

'After doing the army assault course, I fell in the water and had a mud fight with Mel B. We really mucked around – tipped water over each other and rolled around until our bodies, clothes and hair were caked in mud. Geri joined in, too, and got covered!'

Victoria: 'I chose everything I wear in the film. There was one thing that I didn't want to wear because I looked absolutely gross in it – a silly, horrible, disgusting unflattering army dress. But I wore it anyway. Apart from that, I liked my movie wardrobe. Geri always knew what she was wearing in advance,

but the rest of us didn't. A lot of the time we didn't actually know what we were wearing until we turned up on the day, but that's all part of it.'

Mel B: 'It was great doing the assault course with Michael Barrymore. We were all in army gear and we had to run along the course and swing across some water. We weren't supposed to end up in the water, but we all eventually did. It was very funny, although I was a bit scared of dislocating my knee like I did at school.

'One day we had to jump off a platform and do a forward roll in the air – as if we were falling off a bus. That was quite energetic. You had to say to yourself 'Come on!' and then just do it. Often if you stop and think about what you're doing, it can freak you out a bit.'

Hanging Around

Mel C: 'There was always stuff to do when we were waiting around to go on set. Whenever we've got a spare five minutes we sign loads of photographs, because people always want them for charities and stuff like that. So we just sign and sign and sign. We also have to approve pictures of ourselves and cross out the ones where we look ugly. 'No! No one can see me looking like that!' Somehow we managed to fit in loads of interviews for magazines and photo shoots, too.'

Mel B: 'At first it was very boring hanging around to do scenes. They often told us we had half an hour to go, but really they meant an hour. But I soon got the hang of making the most of my free time. I went shopping a few times. One day I got World of Leather to open up for me during one break.

'I took my cat to the studios quite a few times. It was comforting and soothing to have a little animal around. I made everybody give him lots of loving so that he wasn't left alone.

We even made Dean the photographer give him a little photo-shoot so that he could be in on it all and experience what my life's like. One day he jumped out of the window and nearly killed himself. I saw him on the other side of the window and I called to him. He looked at me and then just fell off the ledge. I didn't dare to look down in case he was lying there splattered. Apparently cats fall really well, so he was fine.

'In the trailer, we spent most of the time eating round a little table, having a laugh or sleeping.'

Emma: 'I've become a lot more patient since we did the film. We had to wait around a lot. We'd get there at 6am and get ready – then it would rain when we were meant to be shooting an outside scene and we'd have to wait until it stopped. It was like: "Right, well I've been here since six o'clock in the morning and it's now twelve o'clock in the afternoon. Grrrrrrr!" So you become very patient and start discovering things you like doing

'Soon I got the hang of making the most of my free time. I went shopping a few times. One day I got World of Leather to open up for me during one break.' *Mel B*

– like reading or watching early-morning programmes.

'I watch films in a completely different light now. Straight after we finished our film I couldn't watch anything without thinking, "I bet he didn't mean to do that," or, "I wonder how they did that effect," or, "how many times did he do that take?" You become much more aware of behind the scenes and how much work goes into filming. Once you get past that, you appreciate a film so much more.

'I think maybe when we get dressed up for the premiere and walk along the red carpet knowing that everybody's here to see our film, then we'll feel like movie stars. But when you're in make-up looking like a pig-dog in the morning and someone's telling you that you've got to be on set in five seconds, you don't feel at all glamorous. I often sat there thinking, "I couldn't do this all my life." We worked very hard and there were lots of not very glamorous moments, like falling asleep on the sofa, or doing an army assault course.

'Sometimes we'd start at 6am and finish at 6pm – or 7am until 7pm – so then we'd have the evenings free and I'd spend some time with my mum or see a couple of my old friends. But sometimes I was too tired to do a lot and it was nice to go home, get into bed, watch a bit of telly and chill out.'

Victoria: 'I didn't really feel glamorous on the film. It looks really glamorous, but in fact you're sitting around for hours and hours and there were a lot of early mornings and late finishes. It's just something you have to do, though. I've become a lot more patient, because I got so used to hanging around all day. In my spare time, I ate loads of cherries and mangoes and drank Diet Pepsi. I did actually enjoy it, though, and I'd love to do it again.'

Mel C: 'I didn't have much of a social life during the making of the film. It was quite a social thing seeing the crew every day and chatting with our make-up and hair people, Karen and Jenny. We liked everyone who was working on the film. They were all really nice. But we were working fourteen hours a day most of the time, so when we weren't on the film, we were in bed. It was filming, bed, get up, filming, bed, get up – every day.'

Mel B: 'No matter what I do, I always have a social life. That's what keeps me sane. I had a couple of mates down on set and my sister came down, too. I think it's really important to keep up with your mates even when you're working such long hours. Some days it's not possible because you're literally exhausted, but then there's always the telephone.'

Friday, 4 July
TOP OF THE POPS
We filmed the Walkers Crisps advert at some film studios where we happened to bump into Gary Oldman. He was lovely and down to earth. We met his eight–year-old son, who is a big fan and we asked him to be in the party scene in the film. Fingers crossed – it would be wicked.

We also decided to use our new song, 'Too Much', at the opening of the film instead of the Pepsi track. This is a fantastic idea because we wrote it on the set. It's such a sad ballad that it will surprise everyone.

Saturday, 5 July
Today we filmed the last scene of the film, where we realise the audience is still watching after the credits roll. It was a bright sunny day and most of the cast were there. Everyone was on good form. We met the guy from *Saturday Night Live* – he plays a writer in the film and seemed pretty good at the part.

What a difference it makes when the sun shines.

Sunday, 6 July
We were shooting at Chelsea and Westminster Hospital – the most expensive rebuilt hospital in England. It looked rather like a sports centre.

A long day – we started at 10am and didn't finish until 1am – which involved running down corridors chasing the bad guy (Richard O'Brien), an intimate bed scene with a sick patient and banter with the *Peak Practice* doctor. We stopped by the children's ward to say Hi! Seeing those brave kids smiling through their pain was the most inspiring part of the day.

The last scene was at 12.30am. Okay, a close-up. So I get a hair and make-up touch-up and I'm ready to go. Oh no, it's only a back shot!

Monday, 7 July

At the Top of the Pops studio – talk about organised chaos. After writing 'Too Much' last week when we were in the Docklands, we decided we should have it as the opening song in the movie. This was only decided two days ago, so this morning we're in our winnie working out our choreography. Talk about last minute!!!

But let me tell you, I know a monster when I feel one, and performing this today certainly gave me the shivers – it felt soooo good. We went for the slick white look, so hopefully the classy ballad opening will be a bit of a surprise start to the rollercoaster...our movie!!

Mel C: 'I loved the day we did the *TOTP* scene and sang "Too Much", one of our new songs. I think that it's my favourite song on the album, actually. It was great – I felt like a proper pop star, looking at the camera and giving it loads.'

Emma: '"Too Much" always reminds me of the months we were making the film. We wrote a lot of the songs on our new album around that time. We were having fun because we were all together and having a laugh and running around doing different scenes. So the vibe was always good when we went into the recording caravan at night to write songs. And the songs just come together when we're vibing and having a laugh.'

8-9 July

OUT THERE- ALIENS!!
They're here... In a misty forest somewhere on the outskirts of Slough Burnham Beeches, we met another life force.

It was freezing cold. We endured red ants, a wind machine

and the bite of evening chill until 4am. I wasn't comfortable in my PVC. This is a really excellent scene. It was nearly left out of the final draft – thank goodness it wasn't. We played that game of would you rather eat a live sparrow or a spider? A poo or a glass of wee?

Saturday, 12 July

The break-up of the Spice Girls – a tense scene at the Albert Hall where we tell Clifford to get lost and there's bickering between us. It's quite ironic – the mood of the scene was quite similar to our own: angry, tired and defiant.

The honeymoon period is over and we and the crew are getting rather snappy. But hey, it's like a summer romance – fun while it lasts.

Mel B: 'When we had our argument scene it was easy, because I just flicked on to that part of me and brought back the feelings of when I was last angry. It really was easy. Maybe that's because my life is one big drama. Us five do argue occasionally. It's only natural when we're together all the time, but it's never anything serious.'

Emma: 'We'd known Kim Fuller, the writer of the film, for quite a few years, so he knew what we'd do in certain situations and how we'd react to things. He's a friend, so he knows exactly what we're like and what we say and how we'd argue, so that was cool. We sat down and went through the script and if one of us said, "No, I wouldn't say that," he changed it. I think the best scenes were the ones when we're all together, chatting or having a row.'

Performing

Live

Mel C: 'The scenes I enjoyed the most were the ones where we were performing. The day we shot the Albert Hall scene was absolutely amazing. It was ace – the atmosphere was electric. Getting up on stage is the best feeling in the world – it's what the Spice Girls are all about.'

Emma: 'Just before we went on to do a scene that was weird or mad or difficult, we'd hype ourselves up by marching and punching the air.'

The Albert Hall scene, where the Spice Girls perform live to their fans for the first time ever, is the climax to the film.

Sunday, 13 July

Albert Hall extravaganza. 4,000 people, a monumental building, a mad film crew, five girls and a crackin' new number. I can hardly believe it – the vibe was electric. Just another day on set,

not quite. Today was the peak of the movie shooting.

After hours in make-up and hair and lots of general neurotic manic activity we arrive on set, only and hour and a half late. The crowd whipped up into a frenzy. We performed 'Spice Up Your Life' five times. It felt pretty good and the crowd were really receptive considering they'd never heard it before. We managed to wing our dance routine to slickness.

There are no words to describe how it felt performing. I guess you have to be there, inside one of us, to feel it. But it's complete emancipation, liberation and freedom. It's gratifying receiving that warm adoration. One could almost bask in that intensive electrifying vibe, just like the sun.

We kept up the compereing between takes with the usual banter, followed by a Mexican wave. We managed to cram in two interviews for the US as well.

Energised, we performed three of our hits as a crowd 'thank you'.

Mel C nearly got pulled off when we all got mobbed as the stage was invaded by the fans. I quite liked it. It just feels like it's part of a ride that's climbing higher and higher.

Mel B: 'I really enjoyed the Albert Hall scene because it was performing and that's what it's all about, really. Forget all about your interviews and meeting and greeting people – at the end of the day people want to see you getting up there and performing the music that they like. That's 100% important to me.

'It's on stage that your own personality can come out. A prime example is Mel C – she may seem really quiet, but when she gets up on stage she lets it rip. That's what it's all about.

'I designed the outfit for that scene myself. It was a cross between Salt-N-Pepa, a bit of a wild cat and me. I wanted that wild look, but with a different feel. So I went for animal print, but with spots instead of stripes. I hadn't been down the dalmatian road up until then. I told the wardrobe lady Eleanor what I wanted, she measured me up and they made it. It was just how I'd envisaged it – and if it hadn't been, I would have sent it back! I chose everything I wore in the film. Well, I wasn't going to wear anything that I didn't like, was I?'

Emma: 'It seems really silly, but every time I sing "Mama" I cry. We did it at the Albert Hall for the film and I was looking up at my mum and crying, because it was about us. It was quite an emotional moment.

'Just before we did this scene we'd been talking about the tour and I was worrying that I might not be fit enough to do it. But that day we were there for six hours doing the dance routines, singing and chatting to the audience without stopping, and I realised that if I could do that, the tour wouldn't be a problem. The adrenaline keeps you going.'

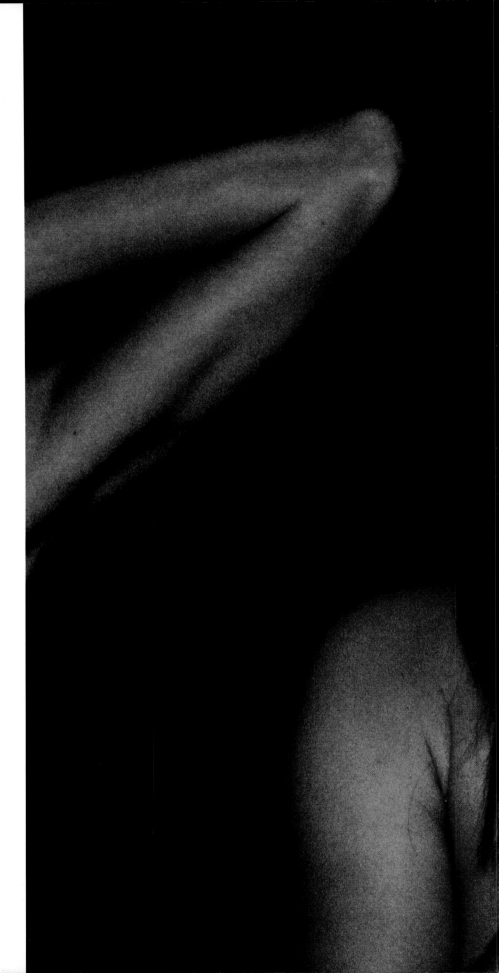

'The day we filmed our concert at the Albert Hall was the best day on the film for all of us, I think. It's such a great feeling getting up on stage and putting a smile on people's faces.'

Victoria

Having a Party

The party scene is set in a fashionable restaurant. Like the press conference, the party is a publicity stunt to plug the live concert. So it's business as usual for the Spice Girls as they speak to Piers (Alan Cumming).

 Piers: (to camera) *Now the big questions – how are relationships moulded in this kaleidoscopic world?*

Piers: (to the girls) *So – do you have any time for boys?*

Mel C: *What are they?*

Mel B: *The thing about men is, right, they should be wheeled in whenever you want one.*

Emma: *You should be able to order them – like a pizza.*

Victoria: *Yes, right –* (miming telephone) *can you send round a deep-dish Brad Pitt. Twelve-inch diameter.*

Mel B: *No cheese.*

They laugh.

Piers: *You do like boys though, don't you, Geri?*

Geri: (laughing) *Is the Pope a Catholic?*

Monday, 14 July

The party scene, in Chiswick. All cooped up in our winnies, squashed inside a large car park. It's the celebrity party scene, only it's now called just 'party' because, although we do have a fair amount of celebs in the movie, they are a bit thin on the ground in this scene. Unfortunately Gary Oldman was too busy, but Jennifer Saunders and Bob Geldof came down and they were both a hoot. Saunders played her 'Edina' part with Victoria and Geldof got the Scary Spice treatment.

There was a lot of hanging about. Mel B is sick, so she went home early.

I wore another understated outfit, which was a celebration of the Renaissance and a tribute to Dangerous Liaisons, with a splash of (fake) Westwood. It was a bustier bask with a bustle and boots and a large feather trimming.

Afterwards we all went to the studio and started 'Lady Is A Vamp'.

Mel B: 'I designed the zebra suit that I wear in the party scene – William Hunt made it for me.

Tuesday, 15 July

The second day of shooting at the celeb party in which Emma and I each had our little moments with a guest. Emma's was a rather dashing actor, Jason Isaac, who was playing an intense writer like Irvine Welsh. My scene was with a very cute guy

called Craig Kelly. He'd just come from filming The Titanic, so they were both 'real' actors!

I nearly got off to a shaky start with Craig. As I walked into wardrobe I thought he was the new assistant and was about to ask him to tie my necklace on when he was introduced as 'your handsome man'. Oh, right!

The filming went really well. Loads of extras. I didn't do too badly and was handed a card by a rather good-looking man. 'My telephone number is on there – ring me. But if you're going to throw it away, don't throw it on the floor!'

'What? Okay, right.'

I was then approached by a girl who said, 'You don't know this yet, but I'm gonna marry you.'

'Okay, fine.'

So that was that. A competition winner came down for a hair cut and red mousse. He was very sweet and only fifteen.

 EXT. ALBERT HALL, DAY

For the press conference, a small podium has been erected, around which a crowd of (real and acting) press photographers congregate. A large banner reads: 'Global Spice Live'. A DJ (played by chatshow host Jonathan Ross) stands by the microphone.

DJ: *And on Saturday the Spice Girls are doing their first live performance here at the Albert Hall.*

DJ: (to girls) *How do you feel about it?*

Emma: *It's going to be brilliant. We'll be singing with a new band.*

Victoria: *And it's being broadcast live all round the world.*

DJ: *In how many countries?*

Mel C: *Millions.*

Mel B: *Maybe more.*

Wednesday, 16 July

Today we filmed the press conference and the bus run with the police.

We had an early start to run over our lines with Jonathan Woss (who can't pronounce his 'R's) before we did our little verbal spectacle in front of the media. In this scene we are announcing the 'Spiceworld Live Performance'.

This was a breeze. Jonathan was very charming with his weally weally good wendition of a DJ interviewing us. We spiced him up in our usual manner.

We met his children and his little two-year-old son was gorgeous, wearing a very cute floppy indie haircut. We certainly have met some great kids on this movie – it's unbelievable how many different characters there have been, which certainly says something about their celebrity parents. And every child

has so much influence on their parents – it's the Achilles heel.

Later we did some bus-running scenes where we encountered the old bill. The actor playing the main copper brought his child along. She was a funny little thing – not an obvious beauty but with such a charming sweet soul that she was a real treat to have around. She was even correcting her dad's lines when he got them wrong. She was only eight – very cheeky, yet polite.

While waiting around between shots in a big Shogun Range Rover, the five of us were alone at last, for the first time in ages. We giggled about how funny it would be just to drive off. Well, I was in the driving seat and then I was actually asked to move the car. So I took it a little bit further round the block. What a laugh! It gave us just that little bit of spontaneity. It's quite sad, I know, that such a small thing could give us such a sense of fun (knowing the security risk and panic it caused), but I didn't think about it till afterwards. It just gave us that feeling that we were still that fab fivesome, all in it together, although security gave me a real telling off when we got back. You just don't realise your actions can affect so many people. They could lose their jobs over something like that.

Thursday, 17 July

DELIVERY DAY!!!

Today we were in the old maternity wing of Queen Mary Hospital. In this scene, our old friend Nicola (played by Naoko Mori, who is fabulous) is having a baby. The tension was

mounting. Moki was great – legs spread, puffing and screaming. There was slapping, fainting, tears and laughter all round.

The baby provided was two weeks old and looked like a real bruiser. Only problem was, he had blond hair. So we had to colour it black to look authentic. The only other problem was that the baby was meant to be a girl and it was a boy! So we kept the giveaway parts well hidden. A very rewarding scene.

Later we visited two little boys who had severe burns – one because he'd been playing with a lighter. It was tragic that such a silly accident could do such a monstrous thing. But in their eyes you could see beautiful brave children who were glad to see us. Puts things into perspective – another reality check.

Monday, 21 July & Tuesday, 22 July

It's the last two weeks of filming the movie and we're shooting at the Twickenham Film Studios. It's like the comfort part after a real slog, roughing it out on location. Typically, it's now boiling outside just as we come inside.

SPICE FORCE

5

It's the Hollywood scriptwriter (Mark McKinney) who dreams up the Spice Force Five. He wants to make a movie with the Spice Girls as superheroines who save the world.

Wednesday, 23 July

Enter the vixens from hell – the silver Spice chicks who kick ass!

 EXT. PONT DE LA TOUR RESTAURANT, DAY
Writer: *Now this is where the high concept idea kicks in.*
He pauses for dramatic effect.
Barnfield: *Very high.*
Writer: *A US airforce Stealth bomber carrying a cargo of red plutonium is hijacked by a gang of extra–terrestrial terrorists. In the pilot's pocket is a computer disk with the encoded formula of a deadly virus which could destroy the world. The US president only has one option: call in Spice Force Five.*

Kim Fuller: 'With Spice Force Five, I liked the idea that they've all got great skills apart from Victoria, who's just Victoria. Emma doing karate was great, she's great at doing all that. I wanted kids to think, "Wow, that's little baby Spice doing all that." It worked against the stereotype.'

Emma: 'I did a wicked stunt where I had to beat up three male karate experts, throw one of them over my shoulder and another one over my head. I did it all myself!'

Victoria: 'The Spice Squad costumes were excellent. I think we all looked just like mad superheroines in them.'

Thursday, 24 July

Today we filmed the scene inside the bus where we get annoyed with Clifford for booking up our day off with a visit from some competition winners.
'What, no day off?'
Great vibe and verbal banter. We were giving each other serious gip!
See you in the morning.

Monday, 28 July

It's the last week on set – and then it's a wrap. There is an air of anticipation and a little sadness that it's all coming to an end and everyone will go their separate ways. We have established a routine of togetherness – the crew, the stand-ins, make-up, hair, lighting, props etc. And soon the little community will disperse. Eight weeks is a long time to be together day in, day out. But today we marked the occasion with a group photo.
Chris Smith, the Minister of Culture and Arts, came down to the set. Apparently he is the first 'out' gay minister. We spiced him up and I said I hoped he wouldn't overspend on the Millennium budget because there are starving people in Africa?! Barry Norman also came down to film for *Film 97*. He's very funny in his placid manner. We talked about the movie and said that if a film is as good as it feels when you make it, then this will be a great movie.
We filmed the title sequence – a bit of a mix between Tales of the Unexpected and James Bond – silhouettes with long arms and bodies moving.

Tuesday, 29 July

It's really hot and I need a fan. We did a scene today when a little girl is meant to come in screaming. But this little girl merely whimpered. It was hysterical. We're all rather tired.

Thursday, 31 July

Bus sequence, with falling off the bus stunts. Emma and Mel C had stunt doubles. I did my own stunt and fell through the roof. But then we all had to do roly-polys in mid-air as if we were free-falling through the roof. Everyone did it great except me – I tried too hard and ended up landing on my neck. Ow!

Messing Around

Victoria: 'We had a laugh on set like we always do, wherever we are. Of course you have days when everybody's feeling grumpy and other days when you're all in a good mood. When you're feeling good, you laugh and find it really funny if you can't get your lines right. But if you're in a bit of a mood, you get the hump with anyone who gets it wrong. You think, "Oh come on, just get it over with so we can wrap."'

Mel C: 'I'm quite a bore when it comes to work because I am "Little Miss Professional Head" all the time. Some of the other girls are really naughty all the time and that gets me a bit annoyed sometimes. If we need to do something I get angry and say, "Come on Girls, we've got to do it now!" We have a laugh and a giggle and we're rude and stuff, but if the director starts saying "Come on, we've got to do a take now," and they won't shut up and sit still and get in their positions, then I have to give them a bit of a shouting at. Actually, we all take it in turns to pull each other into line.'

Emma: 'We messed about quite a lot. There were some times when we'd say the lines wrong just to make us laugh. It would come to Take Two and we'd say completely different lines to Take One and the cameramen would be screaming, "What are you doing?"'

Mel B: 'I messed around a lot on set and had quite a laugh with the crew. I got quite a few giggle fits, especially when I got my lines wrong. Who messed around the most? I suppose every one of us would say, "It wasn't me!" but I think we're all just as bad as each other.'

Emma: 'Mel B gets the Gumbo of the Film award, because she always got her words wrong! Not really. Sometimes we'd just crack up and wouldn't be able to do a take again because we'd be silly and then when we tried to do it again seriously, we'd remember the silly things we said and crack up again. It would be like, "Oh no! Let's come back to this after lunch!"'

Girl

'A man shouldn't feel intimidated by a strong woman. It's not domination, it's a celebration.' *Geri*

Power

Geri: 'I think the film shows that Girl Power is liberating. It's all about the equalisation of the sexes. A man shouldn't feel intimidated by a strong woman. It's not domination, it's a celebration.'

Mel C: 'Anyone who works with the Spice Girls knows that if we wanna do something, we're gonna do it, but if we don't, then we don't. Obviously everyone on the film had their own specific jobs to do and we really respected that, but I think everyone knew not to mess with us.'

Emma: 'Were we in control? Obviously there were a director and a producer to advice us – and often they know best. But, if we didn't feel comfortable with something, then we'd say so and explain why and talk it through.'

Mel C: 'Everyone's got their jobs to do on a film and the actors do get bossed around a bit. But that's okay, as long as you get bossed around on your terms, with a little bit of respect.'

Kim Fuller: 'The Girl Power theme came out of my observations that, as they've become more and more famous, their friends and the people they've trusted have gradually either betrayed them in a big way by selling stories to the papers or just dropped away. So what has happened inevitably is that the Girls get their strengths from each other and from the whole Spice thing.

'It's so much harder for them to keep in touch with the people they knew at school, because suddenly they're super-stars and can't go to the disco without a bodyguard, in case they get mobbed. So the main theme in terms of their own story within the film is the conflict between them as Spice Girls and them as human beings. As the film goes on, you then get a crisis between fulfilling obligations to friends or fulfilling your obligation to the Spice thing. The Clifford character is driving them ever onwards – as they fight and kick against him, you can see the machinery of stardom at work. Underneath it all, they're basically five girls who want to break away from it all, have a good time, eat chips in the park and be true to who they really are.'

The ALBUM

Emma: 'Going into the studio is one of my favourite parts of what we do. I'd done some singing for TV adverts, so I'd been in the studio before, but it was very exciting doing it for the first time with the band. It's just you and a mike and you're live. When I sing I always shut my eyes to get into the mood and feeling of the song.'

Victoria: 'I'm not very good when everything happens at once, because I just get stressed out. But it was quite good doing the album at the same time as the film because we were always hyperactive after a day on set and that meant we could go into the mobile studio and vibe off each other. We wrote a lot of the songs on the new album during the film, although we had two or three weeks after the film finished to knuckle down and get the last few tracks finished.

'My dad used to be a singer and he got very excited when he heard we were recording at Abbey Road. But for me, because I'm so used to being on the go all the time, I didn't really have time to take it in. We all sang in the studio where the Beatles and Oasis recorded their album, and I think that Liam Gallagher sang into the same mike shield as me because it stank of bad breath. I was convinced that he'd been singing really close to the mike because it smelt so much that I was gipping. Gross!'

Mel C: 'We had a mobile studio on set and we went to Abbey Road the rest of the time. It was excellent there – such a good vibe. Funnily enough, my mum once sang in the studio we were working in. It was a nice refresher to get into the studio. It was

pretty chilled out there – we'd have a late morning. We really enjoy writing and we had the time to go at our own pace.

'We worked with the same people as we did on the last album because we've got such a good relationship with them and we were so pleased with the first album that it felt right to go with the same producers – Matt and Bif and Absolute. They're mates now – we've known them for years.'

Emma: 'When we recorded "Generation Next Pepsi" we were actually in the studio in Abbey Road where the Beatles wrote their album. There was even the original piano they used, as well. I was telling my uncle about it the other day and he was saying that he used to stand outside and look over the wall just to see where the Beatles recorded – and he still does, in fact. I said, "Well I go in there!"

'It's freaky because when you go outside the studio there's a big white wall covered in writing which says We Love The Beatles and Oasis – and then you see We Love The Spice Girls or I Love Emma, and you think, "What, really?"'

Kim Fuller: 'The girls were still writing the album while we were filming, so some of the songs weren't ready and we couldn't put them in. We wanted something strong at the beginning and something strong at the end – which turned out to be "Too Much" and "Spice Up Your Life". There aren't that many songs in the film because I didn't want to lose too much of the story by just going from one song to another. And we didn't just want to replicate the album.'

See Ya!

Victoria: 'I was quite relieved when it was all over because a lot of the time we had to wear the same clothes every day and that was a bit of a drag. Also, we had to get up early and have our hair and make-up done for hours – I suppose we do that anyway, but usually it's for different things. So I was quite glad to move on to the next thing, but it was still sad to say goodbye to everybody because I did have a good time and enjoy myself.

'I'd love to do it again. I'd like to take on a real character that's totally different to me – as long as it's glamorous. I'd like to take on a more glamorous part – definitely nothing less glamorous. It might be nice to be the next Catwoman, in a skin tight suit. I could "cat" a lot and crawl around the floor a lot and be very sexual.'

Geri: 'Making the movie felt like giving birth to a baby. If anyone had asked me to make another film immediately after we'd finished filming, I would have said no. But as time goes on you forget the pain and think, yes, I'd do it again. I'd like to do something more introspective and based more on human behaviour next time.'

Mel C: 'The thing with Spice Girls is that all our dreams have come true. We think that if there's anything in the world that you can imagine you want to do, if you really want to do it, you can. We wanted to be pop stars and we were, so we thought, all right then, let's be movie stars as well! If you don't have a go, you never know.

'I've learnt not to have expectations about anything – you've just got to take things as they come. And we always believe that if something's not a laugh then it's not worth doing. It was a gruelling schedule on the film but it was worth it. When it was over, we all thought, "Yeah! We'd do that again!"'

Mel B: 'At the end of the film I felt pleased and chuffed. A big pat on the back for everyone. Hopefully the film will appeal to anyone and everyone. Film is like music in the way that it gathers all kinds of people together. It's a people's film. You have to go and see it first before you label it.'

Mel C: 'I hope the fans like it. The audience will probably be quite young, but there are underlying jokes and innuendoes in there for the grown-ups. With any luck it'll make everyone chuckle a bit.'

Emma: 'I think the film will appeal to children a lot, but there are also loads of funny bits in it for adults, plus great actors like Richard E Grant, Richard O'Brien and Roger Moore. It's very busy and active, so even if you don't like the Spice Girls, you'll enjoy it because we're not in your face all the time

in every scene. We've always said that everything we do should work on different levels, a bit like *The Simpsons*, where there's this colourful edge and they're very funny, but there's an underlying sense of humour there, too. I'm sure my nan will love it because there are performances in it, and she loves that.'

Friday, 1 August
It's all over! Phew!

CAST LIST

EMMA   Emma Bunton
GERI   Geri Halliwell
MEL B   Melanie Brown
MEL C   Melanie Chisholm
VICTORIA   Victoria Adams
CLIFFORD   Richard E Grant
DEBORAH   Claire Rushbrook
DENNIS   Meat Loaf
NICOLA   Naoko Mori
PIERS   Alan Cumming
JUDGE   Stephen Fry
JACK   Devon Anderson
EVIE   Perdita Weekes
DREAM BOYS   The Dream Boys
DAMIEN   Richard O'Brian
KEVIN MCMAXFORD   Barry Humphries
BRAD   Jason Flemying
FASHIONABLE WOMAN   Jennifer Saunders
RECORD PRODUCER   Jools Holland
BRIAN   Bill Paterson
PHOTOGRAPHER   Dominic West
TV DOC. CAMERAMAN   David Fahm
TV DOC. SOUNDMAN   Steve O'Donnell
CHIEF   Roger Moore
WRITER   Mark McKinney
MARTIN BARNFIELD   George Wendt
ELVIS COSTELLO   Elvis Costello
DANCE TEACHER   Michael Barrymore

LIVE BAND
Michael Martin
Fergus Gerrand
Andy Gangadeen
Paul Gendler
Steve Lewinson
Simon Ellis

DEAN FREEMAN is an internationally recognised photographer whose credits include: cover shoots with Liz Hurley and Dennis Hopper; album covers for Morrissey and Take That; international advertising campaigns for Coca Cola and Levi's; and his own travel reportage projects. He is a member of the British Association of Photographers and is represented in London, New York, Paris, Frankfurt and Milan.

Dean was given unrestricted access to the Spice Girls on and off the set of *Spiceworld* and his reportage images include the Spice Girls in their trailers and make-up rooms, at the Albert Hall and at Abbey Road recording studios. He also set up and shot beauty portraits of them in their costumes. So what was it like to work with pop's biggest phenomenon? "Exhilarating and exhausting!" says Freeman.